50
Le
Pr

D1061401

GTON

AUG 2 9 2002

ABINGTON COMMUNITY LIBRARY
CLARKS SUMMIT, PA 18411

LACKAWANNA COUNTY
LIBRARY SYSTEM
520 VINE STREET
SCRANTON, PA
18509

DEMCO

Kids Can Draw

PREHISTORIC TIMES

by Philippe Legendre

Walter Foster

© 2002 Groupe Fleurus-Mame, Paris.
Text on pages 4–24 © 2002 Walter Foster Publishing, Inc. All rights reserved.
Original title *J'apprends à dessiner la prehistoire*, © 2001 Groupe Fleurus-Mame, Paris.

Attention Parents and Teachers

All children can draw a circle, a square, or a triangle . . . which means that they can also learn to draw a wooly rhinoceros, bison, or prehistoric cave! The KIDS CAN DRAW learning method is easy and fun. Children will learn a technique and a vocabulary of shapes that will form the basis for all kinds of drawing.

Pictures are created by combining geometric shapes to form a mass of volumes and surfaces. From this stage, children can give character to their sketches with straight, curved, or broken lines.

With just a few strokes of the pencil, a prehistoric scene will appear—and with the addition of color, the picture will be a real work of art!

The KIDS CAN DRAW method offers a real apprenticeship in technique and a first look at composition, proportion, shapes, and lines. The simplicity of this method ensures that the pleasure of drawing is always the most important factor.

About Philippe Legendre

French painter, engraver, and illustrator, Philippe Legendre also runs a school of art for children aged 6–14 years. Legendre frequently spends time in schools and has developed this method of learning so that all children can discover the artist within themselves.

Helpful Tips

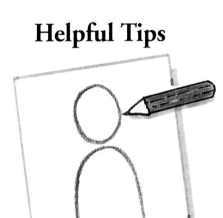

1. Each picture is made up of simple geometric shapes, which are illustrated at the top of the left-hand page. This is called the **Vocabulary of Shapes.** Encourage children to practice drawing each shape before starting their pictures.

2. Suggest children use a pencil to do their sketches. This way, if they don't like a particular shape, they can just erase it and try again.

3. A dotted line indicates that the line should be erased. Have children draw the whole shape and then erase the dotted part of the line.

4. Once children finish their drawings, they can color them with crayons, colored pencils, or felt-tip markers. They may want to go over the lines with a black pencil or pen.

Now let's get started!

Draw two big circles

and tusks in the air

to make a huge mammoth

all covered with hair.

Mammoth

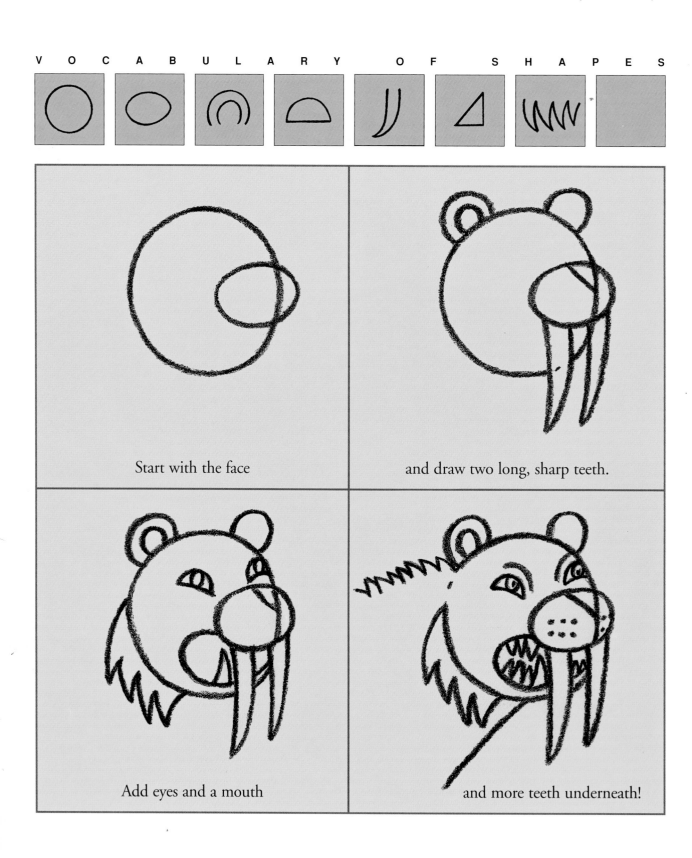

Start with the face

and draw two long, sharp teeth.

Add eyes and a mouth

and more teeth underneath!

Saber-Toothed Tiger

Draw a wild beard

on this fierce hunter's chin

and zigzagging lines

on his animal skin.

Hunter

Draw a large oval,

and add lots of hair.

This rhino was fuzzy—

just like a big bear!

Woolly Rhinoceros

VOCABULARY OF SHAPES

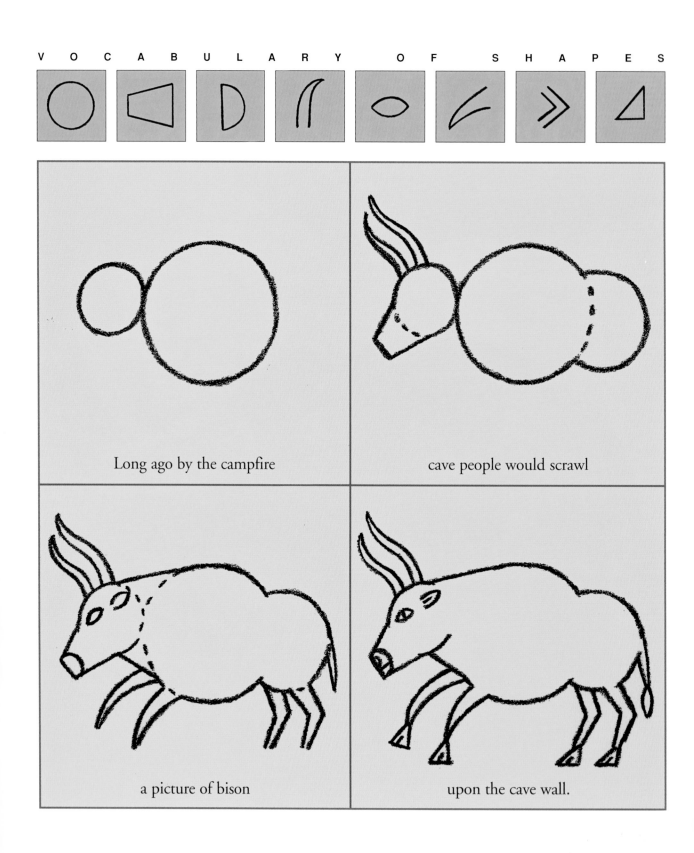

Long ago by the campfire

cave people would scrawl

a picture of bison

upon the cave wall.

Bison

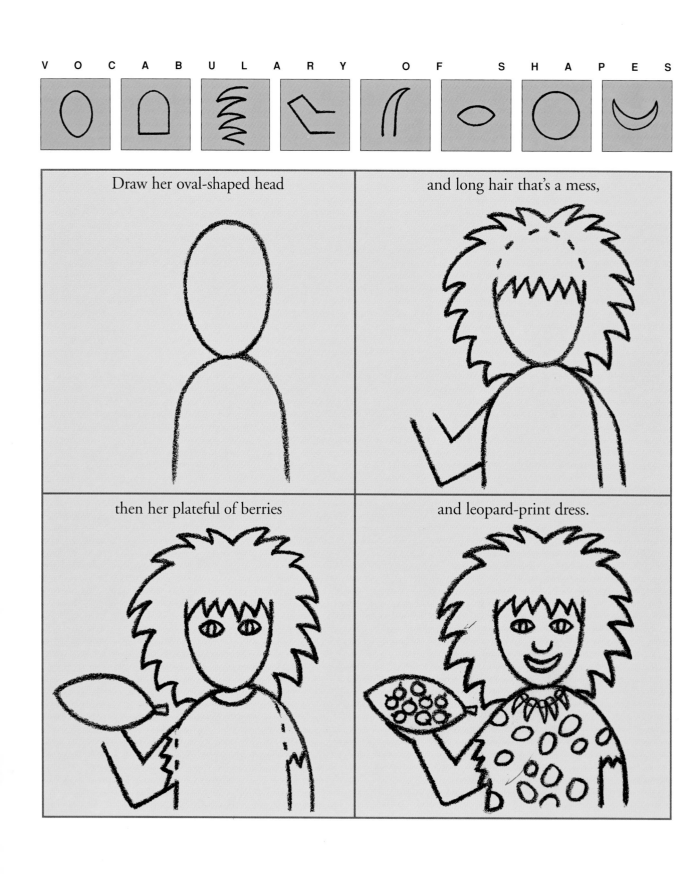

Draw her oval-shaped head

and long hair that's a mess,

then her plateful of berries

and leopard-print dress.

Prehistoric Woman

Draw a rectangle body;

add a circle that's higher

for this Cro-Magnon man

who has learned to make fire!

Cro-Magnon Man

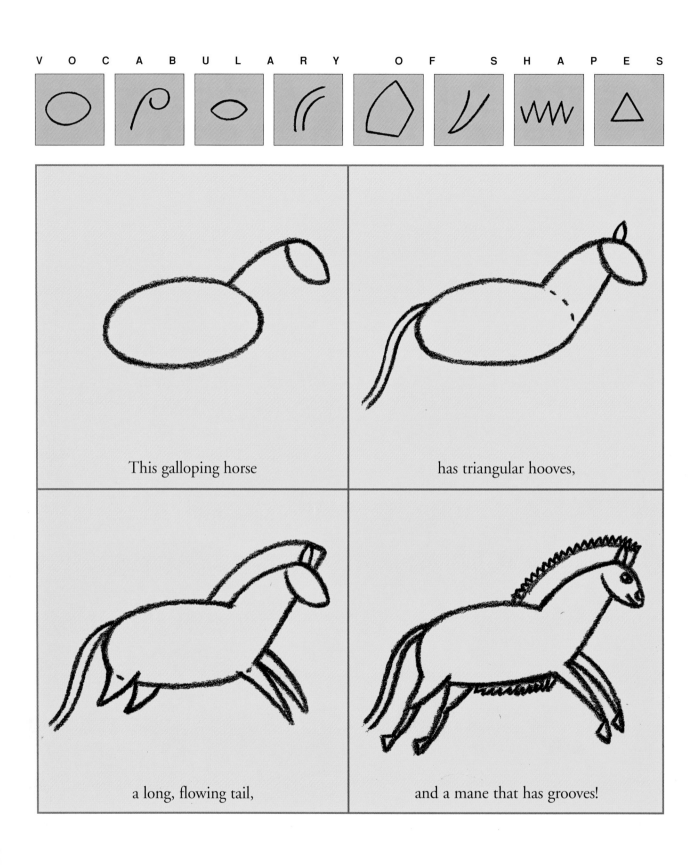

This galloping horse

has triangular hooves,

a long, flowing tail,

and a mane that has grooves!

Horse

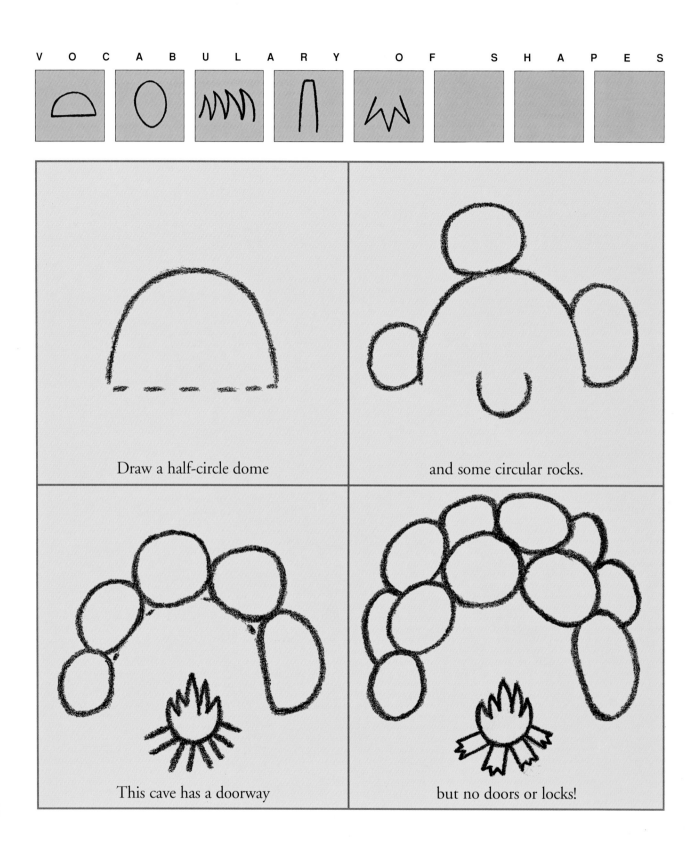

Draw a half-circle dome

and some circular rocks.

This cave has a doorway

but no doors or locks!

Cave

The animals play while the family feasts.

Now draw your own scene of cave people and beasts!